*Lain*

*interest!*

*Elaine Fantle Shimberg*

# GROWING UP JEWISH
# IN SMALL TOWN AMERICA:
# A MEMOIR

By

*Elaine Fantle Shimberg*

*Connie —*

*Good luck*

*always!*

*Elaine Fantle Shimberg*

# Dedicated to Roger B. Natte

*A fellow lover of history, without whose help this book would have had far fewer photographs.*

# GROWING UP JEWISH IN SMALL TOWN AMERICA: A MEMOIR

By

*Elaine Fantle Shimberg*

Abernathy House Publishing

Published by
Abernathy House Publishing
P.O. Box 1109, Yarmouth, ME 04096-1109
www.abernathyhousepub.com

Copyright  2011 Elaine Fantle Shimberg


All rights reserved including the right of
reproduction in whole or in part in any form.
Printed in the United States of America
10 9 8 7 6 5 4 3 2 1
First Edition
P.      cm.

Library of Congress Control Number: 2011938987

Shimberg, Elaine Fantle author - GROWING UP JEWISH IN SMALL TOWN AMERICA:
A MEMOIR


Summary: A young Jewish girl's journey of self-discovery.

ISBN: 97809741940-8-0

# CONTENTS

# ACKNOWLEDGMENTS

This book could not have been written without the input of many of my Fort Dodge classmates and other friends and relatives, such as Roger B. Natte, Fort Dodge Historian; Dave Marrs; Alan Arkin; Marie Killinger; Mimi Swartz Keller; Fr. Richard Graves; Bud Levinger; Sherri Josephson; Sherwin Thorson; Isaac Mallah; Marvin Barkin; Sandy Rogers May; Jerry Higgins; Frank "Butch" Waldburger; Harlene Glazer Lewin; and Georgeann Whittemore Kuhl.

The photos were an important addition as well. Those not belonging to the author are from the Webster County Historical Society archives and photographer Harold Bergeman. The photo of the stained glass window depicting Abraham with Isaac and the Angel is from Congregation Schaarai Zedek in Tampa, Florida. The photo of Sioux City Central High School, "The Castle," is courtesy of the Sioux City Public Museum, Sioux City, Iowa and is used with permission.

As always, my love and appreciation to my children, Kasey, Scott, Betsy, Andy, and Michael and their spouses, and to my wonderful, supportive husband, Hinks.

Note: Parts of the material in Chapters 5, 11, and 17 appeared for one time use in issues of *The Jewish Floridian* between 1979 and 1980.

*"Teach me, O Lord,*
*to obey Thy will,*
*to be content with what,*
*in Thy wisdom,*
*Thou hast allotted to me, and to share Thy gifts*
*with those who need my help."*

*The Union Prayerbook for Jewish Worship*

*The Central Conference of American Rabbis*
*New York 1940*

*My mother and father with paternal grandfather holding me in Yankton.*

# PREFACE

Many people assume that when Eastern European Jews immigrated to America in the late 1800s and early 1900s, they all settled in major cities in the northeast like New York City, Boston, and Philadelphia. The truth is, thousands of them also scattered throughout the United States, often landing in small communities with few, if any, Jews. Often, they made their way first as peddlers, selling as they walked from place to place, and eventually, creating their own clothing stores or grocery stores.

My great-grandfather, Charles Fantle, is a typical example. He arrived from Bohemia as a penniless boy immigrant early in the nineteenth century. He trudged through the territories on foot with a backpack filled with merchandise to sell. Within two years, he was able to buy a horse and cart. In 1836, he founded his first store in Ann Arbor which he ran successfully for fifty years, during which he sent his four sons out to locate communities in which to create additional stores.

One son, Charles, Jr., went to Sioux Falls, South Dakota. Another, Samuel, became a merchant in Hudson, Wisconsin. The third son, William J. Fantle, was my grandfather. Still in his late teens, he opened his first small clothing store in 1883 in Yankton, South Dakota. Ten years later, he opened "Fantle Brothers Big Store." He was joined two years later by his brother, Moses, and the four Fantle Brothers Stores were organized.

Learning from his father, William began to put his two sons to work in the Yankton store as soon as they had graduated from Shattuck Military School in Faribault, Minnesota (despite the fact that the youngest son, my father, desired to continue playing his five-string banjo and accordion in Lawrence Welk's band).

The oldest brother, Willard, soon was assigned to open a new store in Austin, Minnesota and in 1935, was transferred to LaCrosse, Wisconsin to take charge of that store. Harold, a brother-in-law, managed a store in Racine, Wisconsin.

My father, Karl, was trained in all four floors of the Yankton store. He specialized in glassware, kitchenware, drapery, needle-goods, and opened the modern bargain basement. He also handled the store advertising and publicity.

9

*Maternal grandparents, Blanche Hammel Edelson and Morris Edelson.*

My maternal grandfather, Morris Edelson, "grew" his own clothing store as well, beginning as a peddler when he arrived as a teenager from Lithuania in July of 1891. (I have his naturalization papers renouncing any allegiance to the Czar of Russia, therefore allowing him to become a citizen of the United States as soon as possible, which he did.) Grandpa eventually settled in Ironton, Ohio and opened a men's clothing store, "Edelson's Men's Shop."

My personal story is probably no different than those of thousands of other Jews who grew up in very small towns, with no rabbi, and who struggled to have enough for a minion even for the high holy days.

# CHAPTER 1: IN THE BEGINNING

*"I never even realized I was Jewish until I was practically grown up.*
*Or rather, I used to feel that everyone in the world was Jewish,*
*which amounts to the same thing."*
Joseph Heller, *Good as Gold*, 1979

I was born in Yankton, South Dakota on February 26, 1937 at Sacred Heart Hospital at 8:37 p.m., thus increasing the number of Jews in that community to sixteen. All but four of them were close relatives. This kin connection was fairly typical in these small Jewish enclaves where families often were joined by other relatives, giving them all a sense of security. In *Jewish Life in Small-Town America*, author Lee Shai Weissbach quotes Edna Ferber, who upon arriving in Appleton, Wisconsin in the late 1890s, said that the local Jewish community was "a snarl of brothers, sisters, uncles, cousins, very puzzling to the outsider."

Nevertheless, just three years after my birth, in 1940, my father moved me, my six-year-old sister, and my mother away from our relatives in Yankton, South Dakota to Fort Dodge, Iowa, a town of twenty-seven thousand, thus reducing Yankton's Jewish population by twenty-five percent.

By comparison, the Jewish population of Fort Dodge was "enormous." It included thirty-two families, many of them related. Yet, there was no physical synagogue. Although the Iowa Jewish Historical

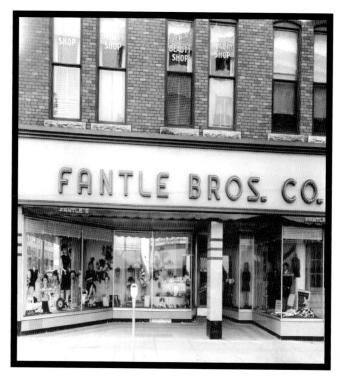

*Two views of the Fort Dodge Fantle Bros. department store.*

Society cites that "Beth El Synagogue in Fort Dodge was founded in 1918," the synagogue wasn't built until 1948, probably because although some of the families were of the Reform or more liberal movement (as we were), others were Conservative, and a few were Orthodox. Since the men couldn't agree on what type of synagogue to build or what type of services to hold, they did nothing (other than debate, which Jews love to do).

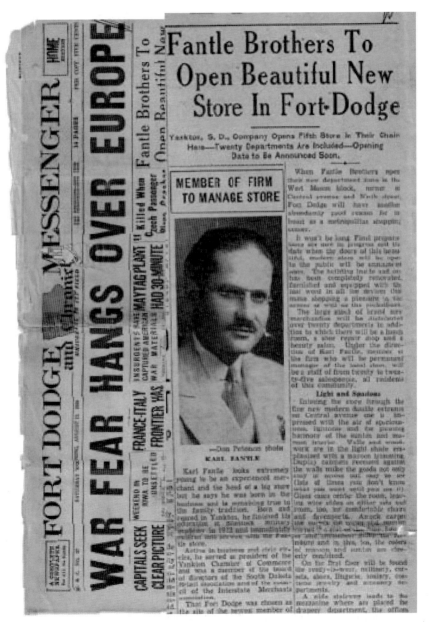

# CHAPTER 2: SURPISE! IT'S A HOUSE!

*"Where Thou art—that is Home"*
Emily Dickinson Poem
(c. 1863)

When we moved to Fort Dodge in 1940, we stayed for a short time at the Warden Apartment Hotel while my father was busy settling the fifth and newest branch of the family clothing store (Fantle Brothers, Famous for Fashions). Daddy called it being in "the rag business" or "the Shmatteh Trade," both common terms (one English and one Yiddish) for women's dress shops.

My only memory of the hotel was standing by the metal railing that overlooked all of the lower floors and spitting to see how far it would drop. I received a smack on my behind for that because my spittle apparently fell far enough that one of the hotel's guests complained that it had hit her on her new hat. (My parents must not have believed in an old-fashioned spanking. I only recall being put across my father's knee once and being spanked, albeit half-heartedly. That infraction was not coming downstairs for Sunday lunch when Mother called. Daddy spanked my sister, Kay, first. I considered running away before it was my turn. I didn't.)

My father soon moved us to a small house on a street with many larger homes. We stayed there only a short time. My memories of that house are picking rhubarb in the backyard that we dipped in sugar and ate and that it had a long sidewalk in front where my sister (Kay, age six) and I (age three) could ride our tricycles as fast as we could in front of all the other houses until we came to the street, where we had to turn around and go back. Obviously, because her legs were longer, she could pedal faster. I, being somewhat competitive even then, decided that the only way I could catch up was to swerve into her. I succeeded in my maneuver. It slowed her down, but knocked me off my tricycle and I hit the sidewalk, cutting my lip and raising a large bump on my head. As my mother put ice on my puffy lip, she scolded my sister for not looking after me better. Yes, sibling rivalry starts early.

*Me on my "demolition derby" tricycle.*

That same year, Kay and I both had our tonsils out at St. Joseph Mercy Hospital on South 17th Street. As the anesthetist, a nun, put the mask over my face to put me to sleep, I kicked her in the stomach. As I lost consciousness, I recall thinking, "I'm going to die. I just kicked a nun!" But I survived.

*St. Joseph Mercy Hospital*

After the surgery, Kay, more stubborn than I, refused to touch the ice cream the nurses brought in to soothe our throats. I happily ate mine and then hers too and my throat healed before hers. I think that began my long love affair with ice cream (any flavor but chocolate).

In 1941, my father had a surprise for my mother. Daddy bought her a new house—an extremely large house standing on a lot approximately 450 feet by 175 feet --without her ever seeing it. Although the house had cost $112,000 when it was built in 1919 by L.E. Armstrong, an industry leader in gypsum and other products, Daddy paid only $5,500, a portion of the taxes due on it. To say my mother was surprised is an economy of words.

The house was 100 feet long, enormous, at least by Fort Dodge standards. The living room and dining room had magnificent oak ceiling beams and the dining room had oak paneled walls. At the top of the dining room wall was a decorative border of cut velvet which I always wanted to touch, but never was tall enough. The living room had imported tooled leather, gold colored wallpaper, hung, it was said by Italian paperhangers who were brought over especially for that task. The same wallpaper was on the walls that followed the oak grand staircase, past the lounge area landing located half-way up and onto much of the second floor where our bedrooms were located. The only

*My family with baby Chuck makes five. I'm on the right.*

other time I've seen that type of wall covering was in Lenox, Massachusetts at an inn called Blantyre.

There also was a wonderful banister leading from the lounge landing to the main floor that we used to slide down when our mother wasn't looking. I once got my knee stuck between the spindles of that banister and we had to get a handyman to remove the spindle in order to release my leg. Mother wasn't amused.

My mother could only see the demands of the house's tremendous upkeep (especially later that year when America was at war, and she had another surprise: my new baby brother, Charles, always known as Chuck to care for). To my sister and me, however, it was a veritable playground.

The house had seven bedrooms, seven bathrooms, and one half bathroom. There was an elevator shaft (although the elevator had not been installed) and bell system that registered in the kitchen to call our non-existent servants. Mother loved the walk-in cedar closet on the third floor. I did too because it smelled so good. The cedar closet was off a large playroom/ballroom whose walls were covered with nursery rhyme paintings, done by an artist Mr. Armstrong had brought in from Germany. It was a favorite place for us to play, especially when it rained or was cold outside. There was also an area nearby on that third floor devoted to what once had been servants' quarters with a small kitchen, bathroom, bedroom, and sitting area.

To my delight, my bedroom on the second floor still had the original wallpaper. Its design included fairies sitting on top of soap bubbles, blowing more bubbles. I never tired of counting the different types of fairies and their bubbles. The ceiling had florescent stars that glittered in the dark at night and lulled me to sleep.

My parent's bedroom, also on the second floor, opened into a large bathroom with separate "his and her" sinks, unusual for that period. Daddy's sink was on the right and I loved to sit on the bathtub rim next to it and watch him shave. There had been a bidet next to the toilet, but Mother quickly had it removed, telling Kay and me that it was a "footbath." The shower, big enough for two, had three sprays on each side. When Kay and I secretly tried it out and couldn't turn the water off, our mother had to climb in, soaking her underwear in order to turn it off. While we thought it was very funny, Mother was not amused then either.

As cell phones were not even a gleam in anyone's eye at that time, we had only two landline phones. One was in the front hallway near the elevator shaft, now a closet, and the other, in my parent's bedroom up two flights of stairs. No one needed a treadmill in those days. Running to get the phone and then upstairs to tell a family member the phone was for them, sufficed. When one picked up the receiver to call out, an operator said, "Number, please." Our phone number was Walnut 3864. Why I remember that seventy plus years later, but can't remember any of my grown children's numbers today, I don't want to speculate.

*Karl, Chuck and W. J. Fantle*

Our basement housed the wringer washing machine and was the terminus of a massive clothes chute that began on the third floor (that we threatened to throw Chuck, our little brother, down to see what would happen. We'd pick him up, laugh when he screamed, and quickly put him down before Mother would come running to see what the fuss was about).

Daddy had a workshop in the basement as well. It was home to his hammers, screwdrivers, buzz saw, jig saw, and baby food jars filled with nuts, bolts, screws, and hooks. There always was one of his half smoked cigars resting on the edge of his worktable as he'd forget where he'd put the one he was smoking and light up another.

Another room was filled with an old horizontal ice cream freezer where Mother froze the side of beef she bought from a local farmer each year, along with shelves containing canning jars filled with cucumbers on their way to becoming pickles, tomato relish made from the products of our Victory Garden, and jars of jams and jellies.

There also was an extremely large concrete area that ran the entire length of the living room and dining room above it combined. It had been intended to become space for Mr. Armstrong's indoor swimming pool. Instead, it became our indoor roller skating rink and a popular hangout for our friends. Later, Daddy built a stage at one end and built a model electric train area, complete with numerous trains, houses, and cardboard and plaster mountains and tunnels.

There also was a scary dusty wine cellar at one side of the basement, filled with cobwebs, not wine, because my parents only drank bourbon and scotch.

*Our house at 775 Crest Avenue in Fort Dodge; note the globe, my "pensive perch" on the lower right corner.*

This rambling house was heated by a massive coal burning furnace. At regular intervals "Vince, The Coalman" came, backed his truck up to the coal chute, and dumped coal into the furnace room. Then he "stoked" the furnace. Not only did we kids have no idea what that meant, I don't think my parents did either, nor did they care as long as Vince, The Coalman, kept the house warm in the winter, which he did. We never saw him haul away the ashes, but I assume he must have.

There was no air conditioning in the summer, but it wasn't needed. The brick walls were very thick and the home stayed cool all during Iowa's often extremely hot summers (although we spent most of our summers at Sunnyside, my grandparent's cottage at Iowa's Lake Okoboji as did my father's three siblings and their families. All of the grandkids slept on cots on the big sleeping porch on the second floor. Daddy, like the other men, came up on weekends, plus two full weeks in July).

Outside the house in Fort Dodge, we had a croquet court in one yard; in another, an old fashioned "tea house" that had wood stacked on one side so we had play space on the other that became our mansion, prison, or hovel, depending on what game we were playing at the time. We planted a

Victory Garden with lettuce, green onions, cucumbers, carrots, tomatoes, and radishes.

I was almost five years old when the Japanese bombed Pearl Harbor and America went to war. Although it changed my life, I was too young to realize just how it was different from before so I followed my mother's instructions. When I found a rubber band, I rolled it around the ball we were forming from rubber bands; when opening a tin can, we poured out the contents, then turn the can over and opened the bottom as well. I got to stomp on the can to flatten it. My sister, Kay, reluctantly gave up her beloved rubber float shaped like a swan and I donated my rubber beach shoes and rubber bathing cap. We helped with paper drives as well. It was part of what they told us was "the war effort."

As butter was rationed, we used oleo that came in a little bag with a yellow dot of coloring. It was my job to squeeze the bag until the yellow coloring was uniform throughout the white oleo and we could call it "butter." The Victory Garden mentioned above gave us most of our vegetables during the war, but I just thought it was fun to pick the carrots, pull the onions, and scare the rabbits away from the lettuce.

I had my own War Ration Book, as did all the family members, that Mother used when shopping for groceries and there were little red tokens

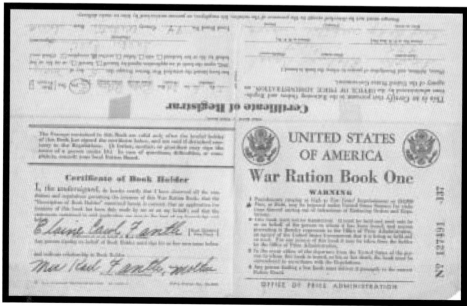

*My War Ration Book, that I received when I was five years old.*

that could be traded in for meat which also was rationed. Sugar was rationed too. One day Mother decided to make cookies for us as a treat. She took the precious bag of sugar out of the cupboard and the bottom tore open, spilling sugar all over the kitchen linoleum floor. Mother stared at it and then plunked down, weeping, her tears washing over the wasted sugar. I didn't know what to say as I had never seen her cry before, so I just crept out of the room.

Most of the news of the war came from the radio, newspaper, and magazines such as *Life*, although whenever we went to the movies, there always were news reels showing the latest battle. Because there was no television, then, I think I wasn't as actively aware of the war as today's kids are, seeing bombing and shooting on the TV screen in front of them.

I had older cousins who were in uniform and my mother's youngest sister was in Europe with the Red Cross, serving with the USO. There was a Japanese prisoner of war camp in northwestern Iowa. Other than murmured gossip and worried looks, especially by those Jews with loved ones in Europe, there was little mention or actual documentation of the Holocaust until the war ended and our military freed the survivors and verified the extermination camps to the world.

World War II was a time when Americans came together as one, putting the good of our country first. Everyone sacrificed. There was a slogan, "Do with less so they (i.e. our military) will have more." Even as children, my sister and I wanted to do our part too. As with most adults, my parents bought war bonds as well. In fact, much of my college tuition was paid for by cashing them in when I was eighteen.

The house had another large back yard with a dog house that none of our dogs ever used, and a giant hickory nut tree under which a few beloved pets, including my pet chameleon (named Clifford, Kayo, Chris, George, Reed, Johnny, Bob Fantle), had been laid to rest. There also was a 100 foot side yard where I played tackle football with my friends until my mother insisted I was too old and we had to play touch football instead.

In May and early June, there were lilac trees with fragrant lavender and white blossoms that lined our circular driveway like guardian angels. Their sweet scent was and still is unforgettable. Just recently, I walked passed some lilac bushes in full bloom. As I inhaled deeply, the scent awakened a forgotten memory in my brain and for seconds, I was a child again playing hopscotch in the driveway next to the lilacs.

Leading from the front door of our house and down to the street was a winding sidewalk, culminating in eight concrete steps flanked by a wall on both sides, each topped with a giant concrete ball. The one on the left was covered with vines, but the one on the right was bare. It was a perfect perch for dreamers, and I spent a great deal of time sitting on it, lost in imaginative worlds. It was what author Madeline Levine described in her book, *The Price of Privilege*, as a child's "internal home." And it was. I felt happy there, content, and free to fantasize and create stories in my head.

We lived in that amazing home at 775 Crest Avenue in Snell Place for fourteen years until we moved to Sioux City, Iowa. Yet, despite all that time, it was always referred to as The Armstrong House or, as overheard once, "The old Armstrong House the Jew bought."

# CHAPTER 3: MARY, THE BABY, AND ME

*"That energy which makes a child hard to manage
is the energy which afterward makes him a manager of life."*
Henry Ward Beecher, Proverbs From Plymouth Pulpit, 1887

When I was five, I began kindergarten at Fort Dodge's Lincoln Elementary School. It was an old building even then, having been the second building constructed as a school in about 1870. (It since has been torn down.) As was common then, it had separate playgrounds and entrances for the boys and the girls. The bathrooms were in the basement, a cold, dark scary place that frightened me, which is why in my early grades I often came home in the winter having wet my snowsuit. (The odor of urine soaked wool drying on the radiator in the front hall is an unforgettable scent.)

*Lincoln Elementary School, now replaced by an athletic field.*

23

The main front steps of the school (eight or ten of them) were concrete and steep. It was long before the disability act. I guess kids on crutches or in wheelchairs stayed home with tutors, as I was to do five years later when I had rheumatic fever and was confined to bed for a year, thereby missing most of my fifth grade (as well as how to do fractions and decimals because neither my tutor nor I liked math).

Catty-corner from the school was Langdon's, a Mom and Pop candy store. They may have sold other items, but all I remember was their amazing patience as after school, my peers and I, clutching a nickel or pennies in each sweaty hand would agonize over whether to choose a licorice whip, a sheet of paper covered with candy buttons, wax bottles filled with a sweet syrup, or a piece of Turkish Taffy. For me, the licorice whip usually won out.

I remember my first day of school vividly because I was so excited to start school. I had been in playschool the year before where my only claim to fame was that I was the only youngster who knew how to tie shoelaces

*Trying to read just like Kay.*

(no Velcro then), but I was tired of playing games and coloring pictures. My older sister was already in second grade and I desperately wanted (and fully expected) to catch up with her. The kindergarten room was on the left as you entered the building. I waved goodbye to my mother without a tear, at least on my part, walked through the play kitchen with dishes and baby dolls and headed back to where the wooden blocks and trucks were. The boys obviously had all the good stuff. Many times the teacher would take me by the hand and steer me back to the little kitchen. When her back was turned, I'd sneak back to the blocks and build tall buildings complete with tunnels running through them.

I also was wiggly during the "academic" part of the day because I already knew my colors, the alphabet, and a few sight words. My mother had bought me a first reader when I exclaimed that I needed to learn to read. It was called *The Home First Reader*, written by Annie Klingensmith, 4th printing in 1936 and published by Albert Whitman & Co. in Chicago. (Pack rat that I am, I still have it!) Now that I have a daughter who's a teacher, I realize how frustrating I must have been to my kindergarten teacher.

*Typical classroom at Lincoln School. My brother is second from the right, second seat.*

As the Christmas holidays approached, my teacher, who probably had taught few, if any Jewish students, asked my mother if I could portray the Virgin Mary in the school Christmas pageant. (There was no thought, then, of making any effort to include the little known and minor holiday of Chanukah.) Mother, not wanting to refuse this obvious ecumenical offer, thought a minute and said, "Yes, of course. After all, the real Mary was Jewish."

My mother, unfortunately, had forgotten that I was an experienced entertainer, having performed at the Webster County Fair as a three-year-old and again as a four-year-old, singing "South of the Border" and "The Good Ship Lollipop" accompanied by my father playing his accordion. Ah, the smell of greasepaint.

Apparently, I did very well in the Christmas pageant at first, smiling at the shepherds as they came to see the baby and pay homage. I patted and then burped the baby, and nodded to Joseph who was picking his nose. Then I must have felt that I was losing the spotlight, because according to my horrified mother, I began to rock the rubber "Baby Jesus" and sing "Rock a Bye Baby," at the top of my voice. The audience laughed and that encouraged me to sing even louder as I bounced the baby up and down. Unfortunately, there was no curtain they could bring down and no hook to grab me off stage, so one of the teachers had to tiptoe on stage as inconspicuously as possible. She whispered to and then yanked the reluctant Virgin Mary off stage. Predictably, I was never asked to repeat my performance.

Years later, I heard rumors that my kindergarten teacher had joined a convent, but I have no evidence and certainly do not accept any blame or credit for that event, if true.

# CHAPTER 4: RELIGIOUS EDUCATION

*"Thou shalt teach them diligently unto thy children..."*
Deuteronomy 6:7

While the fathers continued to debate whether the still non-existent synagogue should be Reform, Conservative, or Orthodox; kosher or non-kosher; music provided by a cantor or organ, the mothers gave up waiting for the men and decided to make their own plans. Jewish women tend to be that way. Despite their differences in Jewish philosophy and tradition, they banded together, united and determined to give their children a Jewish education now. They left the men to continue to argue over what type of services to hold at some later date when they actually had a synagogue.

They rented two rooms for a religious school above Constantines' Restaurant across the street from my father's department store.

*Age 6 with my sister and mother, before a Sisterhood Mother-Daughter luncheon.*

27

The Constantines were Greek, but obviously didn't mind having a Jewish religious school overhead because we were only in session on Sunday when their restaurant was closed. We kids were all fascinated by Mrs. Constantine, who was the cashier we faced when having a soda or cherry Coke after school, because she seemed to have blue hair. Until I was in high school and met other Greeks (both teachers and students), I thought all Greek women had blue hair.

On Sundays from ten 'til noon, religious school was in full swing. The students were a motley crew. We ranged loosely in age from four to fifteen, with gaping holes in many of the groupings. Consequently, it was not at all uncommon for an eight-year-old who read well to be in the Jewish history class with a twelve-year-old who didn't.

The women who ran our religious school were few in number, but they were as determined and mighty as the Bible's Sarah, Rebecca, and Ruth. There was no administrator, no principal, and often, no teacher for a particular class, so we doubled up, the big and the small, reminiscent of the one room schools of yesteryear.

Although we never had actual desks, I recall all of us from ages four to fifteen, sitting on rented dented metal folding chairs. The big kids leaned back and occasionally fell over (causing great laughter among the students and some concern among the teachers/mothers) while the younger ones, like me, dangled our feet and wiggled. The various moms took turns teaching us from materials sent to them from the Hebrew Union College (HUC) in Cincinnati, a Reform institution whose mission was to educate young men (no women then) to become rabbis. HUC was the first rabbinic training school in the United States, founded in 1875. Although the loosely formed congregation in Fort Dodge couldn't afford to hire a full time rabbi, they occasionally hired a retired or student rabbi for the High Holy Day services: Rosh Hashanah and Yom Kippur.

We younger ones colored pictures a lot—black and white outlines of the people we would be studying and talking about like Noah and the Ark, Moses coming down from Mount Sinai with the Ten Commandments, and a scary one of Abraham with a knife, ready to sacrifice his son, Isaac, until God's angel stopped him. The pictures came in neatly packed folders

*Even as an adult, the portrayal in this stained glass window in my temple, Congregation Schaarai Zedek, still bothers me.*

that closed with a string you wound around a button. Every year each student was handed a folder with his or her name on it, containing a packet of pictures to color. I'd peek in, hoping that the picture of Abraham wasn't there, but, of course, it always was.

One year I immediately cut off the string to "see what would happen." Some of the pictures must have fallen out. When it came time to color "Joseph and the Coat of Many Colors," it was missing. Ever resourceful, I leaned over and helped myself to Mimi's. (Sorry about that, Mimi). For months I lived in terror that a revengeful God would shower His wrath upon me. But, by the time I was seven, nothing had happened. I figured He must have had His attention elsewhere on more important things.

Other than teaching us the *Shema* ("Hear O Israel, the Lord our God, the Lord is One,"), and a few other prayers over the wine *Kiddish* and bread *Hamotzi*, there wasn't much Hebrew in our religious school as few of the mothers knew how to read Hebrew. They only knew the above prayers in Hebrew by rote. (It would be years before thirteen-year-old girls would routinely celebrate their Bat Mitzvahs, although in 1922, a twelve-year-old, Judith Kaplan, had celebrated her Bat Mitzvah in her father's synagogue.)

Regardless, these dedicated women were determined to give their children some type of a Jewish education as most of them had come from small towns themselves with few Jews and knew what a struggle it was to maintain a Jewish identity. My mother had grown up in Ironton, Ohio, where there were even fewer Jewish families than Fort Dodge and the nearest synagogue for her family was in Huntington, West Virginia or Ashland, Kentucky.

My brother-in-law, Alan Arkin (not the movie star), grew up in Akron, Iowa with three Jewish families. For many years, every Sunday

29

Alan's mother drove him, his older brother, and sister twenty-four miles over back country roads to religious school in Sioux City on Iowa's northwest corner.

Marvin Barkin's father was a merchant (what else?) in Winter Haven, Florida, where there were just three Jewish families. At age twelve, Marvin traveled fifty miles each week to Tampa to prepare for his Bar Mitzvah. He went by Greyhound bus from Winter Haven to Tampa, then transferred to the streetcar to get to the synagogue.

Over the centuries, Jews had learned to make do with what they had or could scrape together.

# CHAPTER 5: THE SHOW WILL GO ON

*"One's roused by this, another finds that fit.*
*Each loves the play for what he brings to it."*
Goethe. "Prelude in the Theatre,"
Faust: Part 1 (1808)

Although we might have lacked some depth in our Jewish educational program, our religious school more than made up for it with our "presentations." All of our teachers (mothers all) were frustrated writers, producers, and directors. Therefore, even the most minor of holidays was ushered in grandly by a major production. One of the mothers knew how to play the piano and somehow the men had been successful in finding and carting an old grand piano up the winding back stairs from the restaurant. The fact that the piano was never tuned didn't bother any of us. What we lacked in pitch, we made up for in volume and enthusiasm as we sang "Dreidel, Dreidel, Dreidel" (Chanukah) and "Once There Was a Wicked Wicked Man" (Purim) at the top of our voices. My mother was good at writing parodies to familiar tunes so some of our songs had local references, causing our audiences, composed primarily of fathers and grandparents, to howl with laughter.

For two years running, because I was one of the smaller students, I portrayed an ear of corn in the Sukkoth ceremony. There I stood, wiggly because the yellow crepe paper that enveloped me from head to toe itched. The upper classmen (one 10-year-old, one 12-year-old, and one 15-year-old whose mother wouldn't let him quit religious school because she loved doing the shows too much) recited original poems such as "Sukkoth's took us days to build."

The following year I graduated into the pumpkin costume, which had previously been worn by a short 14-year-old who had his own built-in padding. I was quite thin then and had to be "fleshed out" by three pillows tied around my waist. During the reading of the poem, however, the pillows began to slip. By the time the grand finale came (which included some dancing and non-synchronized kicks by the entire cast), I looked more like an over-ripe gourd than a pumpkin.

For Chanukah, I was costumed once more in yellow crepe paper, this time with lettering on each side to resemble a dreidel. I was not asked to repeat my performance the following year, however, due to the fact that while spinning (on cue), I spun off the slightly raised space we called a stage, knocked a baby tooth out and bled all over the three "candles" standing behind the cardboard menorah. Unfortunately, we never had a full complement of nine Chanukah candles (one for each of the eight days of Chanukah and the ninth candle called "the shamas," which is used to light the others) because our school was too small.

The high spot of our Sunday School was rehearsing for the Purim Pageant, as it got us off those uncomfortable metal folding chairs. Purim tells the story of Queen Esther who saved the lives of all the Jews by going to the Persian King Ahasuerus and begging him to ignore his wicked prime minister, Haman, and let the Jews live.

The problem with this story, of course, is that it features only one female in the cast, that of Esther. Every year I hoped that I would be selected to play her. For some reason, I was never picked to be Esther, not even the year my mother was the director, although I came very close. I still think it was politics. Once I almost was Haman. Unfortunately, Jerry, a slightly older classmate, convinced the then director (not my mother) that it was okay for Haman to have a broken arm and I lost my opportunity for unique theatrical greatness.

One Purim I was cast as an ear of corn, wrapped again in yellow crepe paper. Obviously, what the mothers excelled in with their determination and drive, they lacked in creativity when it came to costuming. My sole line in this production was, "I am a tall, sturdy ear of corn." All I managed to say was "I am tall..." As I was well under five feet, the audience broke up laughing. Even at a young age, I couldn't understand why corn (a fall crop featured at the holiday of Sukkoth) was used at a springtime festival of Purim. But of course, we did live in Iowa, "where the tall corn grows."

For the rest of my Sunday School career, which lasted until I was confirmed at age fourteen, I was permanently cast as Queen Esther's guard, dressed in my worn plaid and comfortable wool bathrobe, holding a broom handle, guarding Queen Esther. Always the guard, never the queen!

Today, almost nobody wears crepe paper costumes. Girls can be the king, Haman, or even Mordecai and a guy can be queen if he wants to. Presentations are more polished and more professional-looking, with music and video. Happily, though, for someone who once was one, the corn is still there.

# CHAPTER 6: THOU SHALT NOT STEAL

*"Do not steal, do not deceive and do not lie to one another."*
Leviticus 19:11

The Eighth Commandment says, "Thou Shalt Not Steal." Rabbis say that doesn't mean don't steal "things," but rather "Don't steal someone's reputation," "Don't steal someone's spouse," etc. In other words, God wants you to expand your thinking.

Nevertheless, I have always felt that I had broken that commandment in a small childish, but meaningful, way. I hasten to add that I have only stolen twice in my life, but the fact that I still remember the incidents, reveals their significance to me.

At religious school, we had a small, turquoise tin box with sketches of ancient buildings on it and a slot for money. It was called the *pushka*, which is Yiddish for "little box." Each Sunday we were asked to bring some change from home—usually a dime or quarter—to drop into the box. The money, called *Tzedakah*, was to be used for "those less fortunate than we were."

My sister, a responsible ten-year-old, was selected to act as "keeper of the *pushka*" during the week, so when Sunday School was over, she picked it up and carefully carried it home in a Fantle Brothers shopping bag, putting it on the desk in her room.

As a seven year-old, I felt that my meager allowance really didn't go far enough, especially at the "5 and 10" S.S. Kresge Company store next to Daddy's department store. The turquoise box sitting on my sister's desk was tempting. But I knew it was for "those less fortunate."

It didn't take me long to quickly determine that I was less fortunate than my sister, who had a larger allowance. While she was practicing the piano downstairs and my mother was getting dinner ready, I snuck into my sister's room, turned the *pushka* upside down, removed the metal opening on the bottom that had been sealed with adhesive tape since the key had gotten lost, and grabbed a few dimes and quarters to supplement my meager allowance. I did that a few times and was never caught.

My next foray into a life of crime was three years later and proved to be less successful. While I waited for a ride home after Daddy's store closed, I often stopped by the "5 and 10" store next door to watch the donut making machine. A glob of dough was squeezed out from a spigot and dropped into a section of hot oil. It then plummeted into a series of successive sections until it was fully plumped and cooked and fell into a tray in the glassed-in display case below. I spent my last nickel on a warm donut and continued to wander around the store.

*The scene of my crime: the "5 and 10" next to my father's store.*

I came to the toy section. I had turned the bookcase in my room into a doll apartment house, with each shelf serving as one of the apartments. I was a tenement landlord for my pipe-cleaner dolls. (My sister had a real doll house!) Unfortunately, I was a little short of furnishings for so many apartments and was also short on money to pay for them. Wanting to be a good landlord, I reached into the counter and helped myself to a doll house size pink plastic bathtub and washstand and a set of pink plastic bunk beds. Tucking them into my jacket, I left the store, met my father, and drove home.

*My father, Karl S. Fantle, in his Civil Air Patrol uniform.*

We had dinner at six as usual. I sat at one of the long ends of our ornately carved oak dining table with my father opposite me at the other end. Daddy was handsome in his Civil Air Patrol (CAP) uniform with its wings and captain bars. (I still have them.) He and others in the CAP taught basic pre-flight training at Fort Dodge's Eno Airport, to prepare young men to enter the Army Air Corps and receive more training so they could be further trained in the Army Air Corps to become fighter pilots in World War II. (The Air Force did not become a separate branch of the military until September, 1947.)

My father owned his own plane and had been one of the first to receive a private pilot's operator license when he lived in South Dakota. While courting my mother, he had flown to Ohio to woo her. It must have been successful as she left her family in Ohio, married Daddy, and moved to Yankton, South Dakota.

Usually, I loved watching my father from my end of the table, but this night I avoided his eyes. My sister sat to my right and my mother to my left with my little brother in the high chair between my mother and father. My father mentioned that I was unusually quiet that night. As a toddler, I had not started talking until I was three and I was constantly reminded that once I began to chatter, I never stopped.

*One of my father's first planes.*

Therefore, my silence that night was atypical. Guilt, no doubt.

36

Subconsciously, I must have wanted to be found out because after dinner I went into my sister's room and showed her my new treasures. When Kay asked where I had gotten them, I confessed. She, of course, being the older sister and the "responsible one," told my mother.

Mother calmly announced that she would pick me up after school and we would go back to Kresge's where I would return the doll furniture, admit how I had obtained them, and agree to pay for them from my allowance. I would have preferred a spanking.

True to her word, she picked me up as soon as school was out and we went to the scene of my crime. I was already known to the manager as often when I was there, she'd say, "Elaine, your mother's looking for you." Ah, the perils of a small town. Everyone knows you.

I went up to the manager and opened the bag I had put the furniture in. "I have these…ah, I guess I took them without paying." I pushed the bag towards her. She pushed them back.

"No, Elaine," she said. "I want you to keep these. I want you to play with them and remember how you got them so you never steal again." In retrospect, I now think she and my mother had discussed this plan. I did keep the dollhouse pink plastic bathtub and washstand and the pink plastic bunk beds. I played with them, my children played with them, and now my grandchildren play with them. And yes, I still remember how I got them and have never stolen anything else in the rest of my life. "Thou shalt not steal." It's good advice.

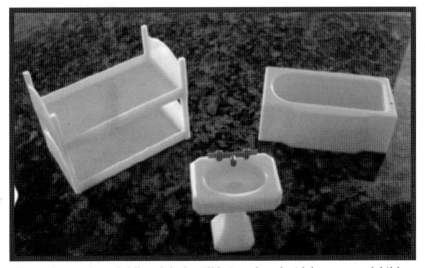

*The evidence of my childhood theft, still being played with by my grandchildren,*
*oblivious to their grandmother's "criminal past."*

# CHAPTER 7:
# WHY THIS NIGHT WAS DIFFERENT

*"There's many a slip 'twixt the cup and the lip."*

Pallada's (FL. A.D. 400) in The Greek Anthology (7th c. B.C.—
10th c. A.D.) 10.32

Notwithstanding the productions we had in religious school, we also were given a smattering of information concerning the celebration of Jewish holidays. We drew pictures of menorahs and knew that Chanukah celebrated a fight for religious freedom and that the holiday lasts for eight days because the little cruse of oil that lit the everlasting light lasted that long. For Purim, we put pebbles in empty clean tin cans to make *groggers* (noise makers) to shake as we booed each time Haman's name was mentioned during the reading of the story of Queen Esther. We ordered "Kosher for Passover" matzo (shipped in from nearby Des Moines) for Passover.

Although Passover is usually celebrated with a home Seder that tells the story of the Jews leaving bondage in Egypt, one time the mothers thought it would be a nice idea to get all the families together for a Jewish community Seder at the nearby Warden Hotel. They ordered *Haggadahs* (booklets with the order of the Seder) which must have come from Hebrew Union College in Cincinnati. Certainly no bookstore in Fort Dodge would have known what *Haggadahs* were, not even my favorite one next to my father's store where I often lingered, agonizing over which of the many Modern Library titles I would purchase for $1.25 each.

As everyone takes turns reading the story of the Exodus during the Seder, they selected one of the men to act as leader and after much debate, decided that all the younger children could recite the Four Questions together, rather than just choosing four children with each child asking one question.

The servers had been given meticulous details by the mothers on how to set the table for the Seder, such as having small dishes of salt water at each place (symbol for tears of slavery), glasses for wine for the adults and grape juice for the kids, along with individual plates for *Charoset* (the chopped apple, nuts, cinnamon and wine mixture that symbolize the cement used by the Jewish slaves to make bricks for their Egyptian captors), a lamb shank, parsley (representing spring) hardboiled egg (circle of life), and horseradish (bitterness of slavery).

However, despite the careful planning and prolonged rehearsals, there must have been a slight miscommunication, as the servers poured the salt water into the glasses along with the wine and grape juice. (I'm sure at least one of them must have commented on the strange Jewish rituals.) One of the fathers, who had been selected to act as the leader of the Seder, said a prayer in Hebrew, lifted his wine glass, took a swig, and spit it out all over the white table cloth and the new outfits belonging to his wife and mother-in-law. It was a Seder I've never forgotten.

# CHAPTER 8: NO PETER RABBIT STORY

*"We never forgive those who make us blush."*
Jean-Francois De La Harpe, Melanie (1770)

Easter was a busy time for Daddy' store. Women came in to buy, not only new dresses for Easter Sunday, but also, fancy hats and new shoes. Both the millenary department and Mr. Benson's shoe department often had standing room only.

As my friends chattered about their new Easter dresses and shoes, candy in their Easter baskets, and sunrise services, I felt left out. Mother decided we'd create our own celebration. We'd have a chicken egg hunt at home.

Kay and I (and Chuck as he grew older) wrote our names on hard boiled eggs with crayon and dyed them in dishes of food coloring. The next morning, we ran downstairs to search for them as they had mysteriously been hidden by someone my mother called "The Egg Chicken." However, she never remembered to count them before she or the chicken hid them and we usually discovered one or two shriveled eggs weeks later under the couch or in the piano seat.

For years after, Mother and I competed to see who could buy the other a package of the yellow marshmallow chickens that appear at Easter. (Now they seem to be lavender, pink, and blue as well.) One year, I won by "cheating" as I saved a package of the marshmallow chicks from the year before and presented them to her in February. She thought that was very funny.

Now that she's gone, I smile, thinking of her when the colored marshmallow chicks and bunnies appear on the shelves.

One year, before our big egg hunt, there was an unfortunate episode. I don't know if it was approved by the Fort Dodge School Board, but when I was in fourth grade, my teacher, Mrs. W., announced that she would read the Easter story to us all during Easter week.

I assumed she was going to read about Peter Rabbit and thought we were a little too old for it. Instead, she opened the New Testament and began to read the story of Jesus and the crucifixion. At nine, I don't think I really focused completely on what she was reading until the girl in front of me turned around and said, "Why did you kill Christ?"

I blinked and muttered, "I didn't do it."

The teacher caught me talking and sentenced me to stand in the corner until the dismissal bell rang. It was the first time I had ever been disciplined at school and I was mortified.

When I went home, I told Mother how unfair it was that I had been punished when I was only answering the girl in front of me. She waved that complaint away as insignificant, furious that the teacher had read the New Testament to her class in a public school. "There is something called separation between church and state," she muttered. She was both a Jewish mother and a redhead. I think that supersedes Mama Grizzlies.

Mother went first to the teacher and then the principal the next day and complained first passionately, and then angrily. Unmoved, the principal said soothingly, "I understand your concern. Tomorrow, Elaine can put her head down on the desk when it's being read." That, and nothing more. Separation of church and state obviously was not a big concern to her as I was her school's only Jewish student then because my sister, Kay, had moved up to Fort Dodge Junior High School.

That was the first time I realized that "being Jewish" made me different from any of my friends. Fortunately, there was no similar experience that I recall while I lived in Fort Dodge.

Florence Selfman, who grew up in Mansfield, Ohio, related a similar experience. She came home from the playground one day and asked her mother, "Do I have a middle name?"

Her mother answered, "No, why do you ask?"

Florence said, "Because some of the children at the playground are calling me "Florence Jew Selfman." That also was the only example of discrimination in Ohio that she recalled. My male cousins, however, who also grew up in a small Ohio town, told a different story of actual fistfights from peers who didn't like Jews—but who really didn't know why.

Mimi (now Naomi), who was confirmed with me, remembered some classmates using the term, "I jewed him down." She said, "Those remarks made me very uncomfortable, but I never said anything because I didn't want to make a fuss."

Basically, those of us from Fort Dodge whom I have contacted in the writing of this book felt there was little, if any, anti-Semitism there and that we and our parents were well-received.

# CHAPTER 9: HOW WE DANCED

*"Dance is the only art of which we ourselves*
*are the stuff of which it is made."*
Ted Shawn Time, July 25, 1955

Although I never learned to dance the hora (there weren't enough Jews in Fort Dodge to form a very large circle), we did have dances. That was thanks to The Young Women's Christian Association (YWCA) "Y" dances for junior high students and Sacred Heart Catholic Church, where they held the Diocesan Youth Organization (DYO) dances on Friday nights for high school students, closely chaperoned, of course. There also were square dances from time to time, held on nearby farms after hayrides.

*The YWCA, scene of the Y-Teen dances.*

The "Y" dances were held on Monday nights. As my father's store was open "late" (until nine) on Monday nights, I would go to his store after school. We'd have dinner at the "Y" cafeteria where we always ordered liver and onions with baked custard for dessert. Then he'd go back to the store and I'd go to the dances—sort of. My friend, Dave Marrs, recalled, "Although the gym was small, I learned to dance there." However, I did not meet with the same success.

Because I was afraid no one would ask me to dance, I hid out in the ladies' room for the two hours, then trotted back to Daddy's store to go home with him. Mother was always waiting to hear with whom I had danced. I always replied, "Oh, lots of people."

Fortunately, by the time high school came around, I was more adventurous. Although most of the dances were the slow dances of our time, many of them included "trap dances," in which a circle of girls could surround a couple dancing and the boy had to select a new partner while his companion had to join the circle. Boys had circles too, but only seemed interested if there were a particular girl

*My junior high photo.*

with whom one of the boys wanted to dance. Either way, couples dancing were closely watched by members of the Catholic clergy who frequently reminded them to "leave some space for the Holy Spirit."

# CHAPTER 10:
# ACTIVITIES, BUT NEVER DETASSELING

*"The quality of a life is determined by*
*its activities."*
Aristotle, Nicomachean Ethics
(4th c. B.C.) 1.10 tr J.A.K. Thomson

We had many ways of amusing ourselves in Fort Dodge, most of which were not organized by adults and were only created with help from our imaginations.

We played Tarzan in the ravine across the street from our home. There was a small creek running at the bottom of the ravine and actual vines hanging from trees that we could grab to swing across imaginary rapids. The mud from the creek was clay-like, so we made clay pots, cups, and plates. Although many years later, my mother said she had never worried about our safety, I reminded her that she had insisted that we only go in threes—"One to get hurt, one to stay with the one who is hurt, and one to go for help." Obviously, thoughts of kidnappers and child molesters were not uppermost in most people's minds then.

We made dolls from Hollyhocks-- large, colorful, fuzzy flowers that grew in abundance around our home. Picking two, we'd turn one upside down and had, until the flowers faded, a doll with a full fuzzy skirt.

Honeysuckle also grew in abundance around our home and we'd pick them and bite off the ends to taste the sweet honey.

In "the interest of science," we captured grasshoppers and put them in glass jars, being careful to poke holes in the metal lids. Then we'd measure how much "tobacco" the grasshoppers expelled before we let them out, or forgot about them and they died.

After a heavy rain, we went out and caught night crawlers, the big fat earthworms that came to the surface seeking a dry spot. These we'd put into a box filled with dirt until it was time to go fishing. My father was a great fisherman and as I adored him, I learned to fish, bait my own hook, and even clean the fish, a chore he hated and conned me into doing by making me think it was a great honor.

There also was the Exposition Pool, an unusual swimming pool

built in 1925. It was built above ground, only one of a dozen or more in the country. We could walk to the "Expo" from our house. During the polio epidemic in the late 40's and early 50's, our mother declared it off limits as she and many other people were concerned that polio might be caught in crowds.

*The "Expo Swimming Pool," built in 1925. It was replaced in 1970.*

One hot day we were bored so we forgot her prohibition and went to the pool to cool off. Upon coming home, she met us at the door and was furious. She had bought us a stack of comic books, feeling sorry that we'd have to forgo the pool. Mother seldom lost her temper and actually yelled, but this time she out-did our father, who yelled often and then quickly forgot why. We were so shocked at her atypical burst of anger that we didn't complain about her tossing our comic books in the trash without our ever reading them.

At least once a year we put on the Flying Fantle Circus. Our cocker spaniel, Honey, was the "lion" we tamed. I did a couple of simple magic tricks, and my sister, Kay, was the ringmaster. What about the "flying?" That was Chuck, our little brother. I'd pick him up and throw him to my sister who, thankfully, always caught him. The circus eventually fell out of favor as our neighbors got tired of seeing the same acts and I think our parents did as well.

In the winter, my father would turn the hose on in the side yard. When it froze overnight, we had our own ice skating rink. It remains a fond memory. Not so fond is the memory of Kay's daring me to lick the curved brass handle on our front door. I did, with the expected results. Mother was furious with her for daring me and with me for being so stupid. It took a lot of warm water on the handle before Mother dared to try to gently pull me off. My tongue was sore for a good week.

We had our favorite radio shows too. We listened to "Fibber McGee and Molly" and laughed each week as Fibber opened the closet door and everything fell out. Little did I know that as an adult, I'd have similar experiences with many of my own closets.

We also loved to hear "The Shadow," when the announcer whispered, "Who knows what evil lurks in the hearts of men? The Shadow knows." The Shadow was a mysterious person who "could cloud men's minds so they couldn't see him." One of my favorite radio shows was "Boston Blackie," originally played by Chester Morris. He was a Robin Hood type of character, a former safe-cracker and professional thief who was, "Enemy to those who make him an enemy, friend to those who have no friends." He wasn't a detective, but helped solve crimes despite, at times, being accused of committing those same crimes. I liked the sound of his voice.

I convinced my mother to buy Shredded Ralston cereal because it sponsored Tom Mix and with a few box tops and a quarter, we could send in and receive an official Tom Mix Decoder Ring. I don't remember exactly what it decoded, but it was a neat ring.

My most favorite radio program, however, was a 15-minute serial with twenty-six episodes that began November 29th and ran every afternoon until Christmas. It was "The Cinnamon Bear," and told the story of Judy and Jimmy, looking for the silver star for the top of their Christmas tree. They meet the Cinnamon Bear, the Crazy Quilt Dragon, and others. Even though we had heard it every year, we hurried home from school and listened to every episode. When my sister and I were adults, Mother found tapes of the original serial and gave them to us. We were delighted, and I was very disappointed that my own children and grandchildren, raised on television, became bored and never got through the second episode.

Throughout the year, the library was one of my favorite haunts. The children's section was on the second floor (added in 1932). I was proud that I had my own library card and was allowed to check out up to ten

*The librarians kept watch for kids (like me) trying to sneak into the grown-up section of the library where all the books looked so much more interesting.*

books. Although I quickly discovered that the adult section on the other side of the staircase had even better books, the librarians kept shooing me away and back to the kids' section. They also kept the "facts of life" books under lock and key so kids couldn't read them without their parent's permission. As no one wanted to ask their parents for permission, most of us received our sex education from listening to the older kids with no way to sort out fact from fiction.

My favorite book, *The Secret Brother*, written by Phyllis Crawford and published by Holt in 1941, was about two kids finding a baby and hiding it in their playhouse. Kay and I played that game in our own "tea house/playhouse" for months. I also read and re-read the *Uncle Wiggily* books that had belonged to my father, as well as *Eight Cousins* and *Little Women*, both by Louisa May Alcott. I've often said that these books were responsible for my wanting a large family, although my husband and I stopped at five.

*The library was a favorite place to visit.*

When it rained, we pulled out one of the ten volumes of the *Books of Knowledge*, a children's encyclopedia set that kept us amused for hours or roller skated in the basement. When it was nice, we played outside after dinner—either cops and robbers, cowboys and Indians, or kickball, only coming home when the streetlights came on.

My father, who loved gadgets, was among the first to get a television set in Fort Dodge. WOI-TV signed on the air on February 21, 1950 and originally was owned by Iowa State University in Ames. They called themselves, "The first educational station in the nation." We sat for hours, staring at the tiny screen on the big console as we watched the process for making jams and jellies with something called pectin and the proper way to milk a cow. We were fascinated by the test pattern and occasionally were allowed to stay up until the station signed off at midnight so we could hear "The Star Spangled Banner" being played.

Eventually, of course, there were more shows and we enjoyed watching "Captain Video and His Video Rangers," the charismatic Bishop Fulton J. Sheen, and "What's My Line" with Bennett Cerf, publisher and co-founder of Random House, and Dorothy Kilgallen, a syndicated columnist, the latter of whom my grandmother said (without proof), wore white gloves on camera so viewers couldn't tell she bit her nails.

There were parent-initiated activities as well. My mother agreed to lead the Brownie group when I was old enough to join. She handed me off to a Girl Scout leader when I aged out of Brownies. I remained a second class Scout throughout my brief tenure there and only earned two badges, although I sold a lot of Girl Scout Calendars. Our leader was uninspiring, to say the least, and I convinced my mother to let me quit. Ironically, as an adult I received a Women of Distinction Award from the Girl Scouts of West Central Florida. They obviously hadn't checked on my childhood history.

When I was eleven, Mother encouraged me to join the Rainbow Girls, a Masonic youth service organization. She was a member of the Eastern Star and Daddy was a Mason and a Shriner. I vaguely remember the initiation, but as I became the "outer observer" and guarded the door, I never knew what was going on inside and again, lost interest. I did, however, keep the pin which recently appeared in the back of my jewelry box.

The activity I enjoyed the most when I was in junior high was meeting my girlfriends on Saturday morning at the Warden Hotel, where we stood outside a large glass window and made faces at the disc jockey, Johnny (one of my chameleon's many names), who was on the other side of the plate glass window playing records on the sole radio station, KVFD (Kindly Visit Fort Dodge).

A few years later, when I was in high school, I was selected to take Kenneth Waterman's then unique class in Radio Speech. We produced the

"Know your Schools" programs that aired Mondays, Wednesdays, and Fridays when school was in session. Some of us also made an appearance on WOI-TV in Ames.

Thanks to Mr. Kenneth Waterman and Ed Breen, owner of KVFD, I also soon found myself on

*KVFD, where I enjoyed my first radio appearence.*

50

the inside of that plate glass window at that same radio station on Saturday mornings giving my weekly gossip program, including such important questions of the day, such as "Who is R.J. dating now?" and "Why did M.P. and S.T. break up?" Yes, it was news, at least for the kids of Fort Dodge, most of whom listened, and probably that was the beginning of my interest in radio (with the addition of television) that became my college major when I went to Northwestern University.

Our newspaper, *The Fort Dodge Messenger* (celebrated its 150th anniversary in 2006) also focused on the local happenings, including writing up many children's birthday parties including the names of the guests, what they ate, and what the birthday boy or girl wore. I had my name in print there often from the age of five and up as my mother, a former newspaper reporter back in Ohio, who considered my parties "news-worthy."

*The Rialto was the "expensive" movie theater of my youth with tickets a quarter. The Strand, down the street, charged ten cents for tickets and had popcorn for just a nickle.*

The movies also played a big part in my life in Fort Dodge and remain so today. There were basically two movie theatres I attended—the Strand and the Rialto. The Strand was the cheaper of the two and ran double feature movies on Saturday. In addition to seeing two movies, you also enjoyed the Pathe News, a cartoon, and a serial, my favorite being *The Phantom* who had a beautiful German Shepherd named Devil. Popcorn was just five cents a bag. There were two other movie theatres, the Iowa and the Park, but I don't recall ever going to either of them.

I was a Roy Rogers fan then and never missed one of his movies, even when it was paired with a Gene Autry film. I cried when Roy's first wife died, cheered when he married his co-star, Dale Evans, and collected every picture I could find of him in movie magazines. I knew his real name was Leonard Slye and that he was born November 5, 1911 in Cincinnati, Ohio.

At age ten, I made a one-way deal with God, praying that I would meet Roy Rogers in person by the time I turned sixteen or I'd stop believing. By the time I was sixteen, I had forgotten all about Roy Rogers (although I remained a believer in God) and many years later, when I was an adult, he came to Tampa, where I now live. I didn't even bother going to the State Fairgrounds to see him in person. Fickle fan, I.

In junior high, the boys took shop and made end tables and wired lamps. We girls had cooking and sewing. In cooking, we learned how to make three kinds of white sauce and "eggs golden rod," (neither of which I have ever made since). In sewing, using a treadle sewing machine which always seemed to go backwards when I wanted it to go forwards, I made a purple skirt and hemmed it by hand. I gave it to a rummage sale, but no one bought it. I obviously had no sewing talent. Kay, however, not only tailored suits for herself, she also knitted the sweaters to go with them.

The age of innocence was fading fast. In 1953, when I was sixteen, the Rialto brought in a controversial movie called *The Moon is Blue*. The Catholic Church's League of Decency had banned it because the word, "Virgin," was used. Naturally, we all wanted to go. Even though a ticket at the Rialto cost more (a quarter as opposed to the Strand's ten cents), my friends and I went to see it. We didn't think it was very good and none of us remembered where the offending word had been spoken.

Summer Sundays, we went to the local bandstand where the band played concerts for a welcoming crowd. It was long before

*Detasseling, one adventure I never had.*

52

*Detasseling was hard work, but teens who did it, had fun and earned good money.*

Meredith Willson's musical, *The Music Man* and we didn't have seventy-six trombones, but it was certainly a popular activity in the summertime. The fact that my boyfriend played French horn in the band was an added plus too.

My biggest disappointment, however, was the activity I never took part in: detasseling. It was a rite of passage for teens in Iowa as well as much of the Midwest and basically, it involved removing the fuzzy tassel at the top of a corn plant to prevent the plant from cross pollinating.

For just a few weeks work, my detasseling peers made a lot of money, at least for teens. In return, they got up before sunrise, took trucks and/or buses to the corn fields, donned sunglasses, hats, jackets, and work gloves and started working by sunrise. Why was I not part of the crew? It was because my mother refused to sign the papers. She said mysteriously, "You never know what all goes on out there."

Naturally, I was curious to know just what did go on. Many of my classmates had detasseled each year during high school, even though they admitted it was hard, hot, and tiring work. The money was good and they said they had fun. It sounded like something I would have liked to have at least tried. I think I'm still a little bit resentful (and, alas, I never did find out just what went on there that was so mysterious!)

# CHAPTER 11: CONFIRMATION CURLS

*"God couldn't be everywhere so He invented mothers."*
Jewish Proverb

The synagogue was finally built in 1948, the compromise being that it would be Conservative, making no one but the Conservatives really happy. In 1951, it was decided that there should be a confirmation ceremony, sort of a Jewish graduation from religious school. Yet, the congregation still could not afford to hire a full time rabbi. As it didn't pay to hire a rabbi to confirm just one student, they hired a retired rabbi named Rabbi Samuel Schnitzer, in order to confirm three of us. The trio included Mimi (Naomi) Keller, ne Swartz (age 10), me (age 14) and Harlene Lewin, ne Glazer (age 16). Harlene's father, Aaron, was president of the synagogue and her mother, Rose, was treasurer of the Sisterhood.

The night before the ceremony, I remember staring into the mirror and wishing I was prettier and "more mature" looking. My straight hair, curled nightly with bobby pins, now hung limply on either side of my head, framing my face like two brown goal posts.

"Maybe if it were a little shorter," I thought, reaching for some scissors. I snipped a little off my bangs. Then I trimmed the left side, then the right. By the time my parents returned home from their movie, I was sobbing on my bed. My hair looked as though my head had been caught in an early model of the Cuisinart. I lifted my puffy eyes up to my mother, "What will we do?" I cried. (Note the use of the editorial "we." I had learned how to place guilt, even at that tender age.)

My mother, may she rest in peace, kept a calm exterior, although years later she admitted that she had wanted to strangle me, despite realizing that it really wouldn't have helped. She looked at what was left of my hair.

"It's short," she said at last. If nothing else, Mother always had a good eye and was a master of understatement. She also was a realist. "We'll have to do something about it."

The years have erased whether or not my relief came from the fact that I could, indeed, still be confirmed, that "Mother will do something," or that I just didn't want to have to return the confirmation presents.

She stood there, staring at my head with its little bits of hair sticking out all over. I looked back at her with tears running down my cheeks. Finally, she turned and left the room, coming back with a box. "Sit in that chair," she commanded. I did. She opened the box and proceeded to make little pin curls all over my cropped head. It was well after midnight when she finished and would it surprise you to know that my father had long gone to bed, leaving the crisis in my mother's capable hands?

"Will it work?" I asked tearfully.

"It will have to," she answered firmly and with the confidence that children have in their parents in times of need, I believed her.

The next morning, she brushed my hair out. It was soft and full, a poodle cut. "If it's good enough for Mary Martin in *South Pacific*, it's good enough for your confirmation," she said.

And it was. I remember feeling pretty adult and I also remember that, with insight that comes only with reviewing memories of one's youth, I never thanked her for "saving the day." I just took it for granted that she would.

On Sunday, June 10, 1951, the three of us being confirmed were all in white dresses and had the burden of reciting numerous speeches since there were only three of us. I got to recite the special "Flower Offering" speech, laying a bouquet of flowers on the base of the ark where the Torah was kept, as well as other speeches on "Our Faith in One God," and "Eternity of Life." Our audience, composed of bored siblings and proud parents and grandparents, bravely sat through the service, especially the lengthy benediction from the rabbi who must have felt that as long as he was there, he might as well give the congregation their money's worth.

All five of my children were confirmed in classes that far outnumbered mine and now, my grandkids are beginning to be confirmed as well. Each time, it seemed, a crying baby sat behind me, with a six-year-old brother chomping gum on one side, and a teenage brother cracking his knuckles on the other side. Yet, each time I fondly recall my own confirmation and give thanks for the continuation, another link between the past and the present, giving hope for the future.

*In 1951, the first confirmation took place, with Rabbi Samuel Schnitzer officiating. The girls included me (age 14), Harlene Glazer Lewin (age 16), and Naomi "Mimi" Swartz Keller (10).*

# CHAPTER 12: SOCIAL LIFE

*"I am a hoarder of two things:*
*documents and trusted friends."*
Muriel Spark, "Introduction," Curriculum Vitae, 1992

Most of our social life in Fort Dodge was simple and compared to today's standards, quite innocent. We attended sock hops (dances without shoes), hayrides, sporting events and cheered our high school team, the Fort Dodge Dodgers. Before football games, we held "snake dances" from downtown to Dodger Stadium, the football field. We'd join hands and snake

*A typical hayride in Fort Dodge.*

around pedestrians and parked cars, running and shouting until we got to the field. The girls had potluck suppers and slumber parties.

I attended the only public high school then; the other high school was Sacred Heart Catholic. Wrestling was and still is a major sport in Iowa so as a group we usually attended many of the wrestling tournaments both at home and in neighboring small communities. I was dating Bruce, one of the wrestlers. I not only attended most of his meets, but also talked him into "coaching" my ten year-old brother for a Y-tournament. My brother was skinny and only weighed fifty pounds. Nevertheless, he won first place in his weight class.

I did not date Jewish boys when I lived in Fort Dodge for the simple reason that there weren't any my age. The only one who had been close to my age was killed in a car crash on his way home from the Indy 500 speed race on Memorial Day. I was fully convinced that I'd be an old-maid.

So I dated Gentile boys, and to my knowledge, there never seemed to be any religious concerns with their parents or mine, although my father did seem pleased when I began dating one young man (the above named wrestler) whose grandmother had been Jewish. "That makes him a quarter Jewish," my father figured. "That would be okay." But marriage was the furthest thing from my mind in high school, although many of my classmates did marry shortly after high school graduation.

My parents' social life in Fort Dodge consisted of having friends over to play gin rummy on Friday nights and going to the Elks Club for dinner and dancing on Saturday. Sunday night, our entire family went to Treloar's Inn for delicious fried chicken and hickory smoked "bar-b-que"

*Trelor's Inn had the best bar-b-que in the world.*

ribs. Other than that, we didn't go out as a family, other than those Monday nights when my father's store stayed open until nine and I went to the Y-teen dances so we had a father-daughter dinner at the Y cafeteria.

The most special dinner of the year for me was the annual Fantle Brothers' Christmas dinner for all of the employees, a common tradition of those days. It was held at Wraywood, a magnificent large home that reminded me of a castle. It had high ceilings and was decorated with numerous giant Christmas trees, lighted candles, flowers everywhere and held an elongated table at which we all sat. My sister and I knew all of the employees by name, although my favorite was an older woman from the millinery department. I'll call her "Hattie" because, although I adored her and would seek her out whenever I went to the store, her name totally escapes me.

Hattie was the one to whom I confided in one day after school as I sat in the millinery department waiting to go home with my father, "I

*I remembered Wraywood as being a magnificent castle. Imagine my surprise when I received this photo and noticed I hadn't been far off.*

know what my watchword will be from now on," I said. I don't think I really knew what a "watchword" was. But Hattie put down the hat she was adding flowers and lace to, and leaned forward.

"That's lovely, dear. Tell me."

I recited a prayer I had found in my Hebrew Union prayer book. It went, "Teach me, oh Lord, to obey Thy will, to be content with what, in Thy wisdom, Thou hast allotted to me, and to share Thy gifts with those who need my help."

Hattie just patted my hand and swallowed hard. "That's a good watchword," she said.

I still remember that prayer and it has directed my life.

I was delighted to be seated next to Hattie that Christmas dinner. She complimented me on my pretty blue velvet dress with the white lacy collar despite the fact that my sister was wearing the same dress, only hers was in lavender. (My mother loved both velvet and sailor suits and as a result, we often wore matching velvet dresses or sailor suits until my sister rebelled.)

A lot of alcohol flowed that night, but I only remember the delicious food that Mrs. Wray served on delicate china dishes and the glorious sense of being in a magical winter wonderland, that and my sense of pride when my father rose to give his usual "We're all one family here" speech. There were a variety of gifts for all of the employees as well as a bonus check tucked into each card. I felt very grown-up and looked forward to this event each year.

# CHAPTER 13: CHRISTMAS

*"All Jews are responsible one for another."*
Babylonian Talmud

There never was a "December Dilemma" in Fort Dodge for three specific reasons. The first was that Chanukah was still a fairly minor holiday in those days and had not as yet become commercialized in order to try to compete with Christmas. There were few, if any, Chanukah cards, wrapping paper, or decorations, other than a thin blue paper streamer that spelled out Chanukah in one of its many different spellings. There were, of course, colorful candles for the menorah that the Sisterhood sold. One box held enough for the entire eight days of Chanukah and, if my memory is correct, cost 25 cents per box. For some reason, we always seemed to have an assortment of candles leftover, probably because we sometimes forgot to light the menorah for a few days.

The second reason that we had no dilemma at Christmas is that like many Reform Jews in those days, we somewhat celebrated the holiday, but in a sort of Santa Claus way. We did have a Christmas tree and each of us had one or more special favorite decorations. But there was never a star on top. Why that made it less religious, I never asked. Mother also forbid us from decorating the outside of the house.

The third reason that our family had no difficulties in the Christmas season was that as my father owned a junior department store, my sister, mother, and I were all commandeered to work Saturdays and evenings as well as over Christmas vacation when all the stores were open. It was a merchant's busiest season. No one said, "Happy Holidays" then, just "Merry Christmas."

Daddy erred in his usually good judgment by initially putting me in the gift wrapping department. I didn't have (still do not have) any talent for wrapping gifts. I cut off too much paper, wadded the ends of the wrapping paper together and affixed them with a great deal of Scotch tape, then covered the entire mess with premade bows. The customers weren't pleased.

Before long, Daddy transferred me to the first floor to sell costume jewelry already displayed in individual gift boxes ranging from 99 cents for a pair of screw-on earrings, to $3.99 for earrings and a matching necklace. I enjoyed the challenge and became quite a competent salesperson. However, once the sale was made, I needed the customer's help in sending the sales slip and the cash upstairs to the bookkeeper's office.

The money was sent in a cup that attached to an overhead container that was delivered upstairs by pulling hard on a cord. It was sort of the precursor to the pneumatic tube. Unfortunately, I was too short to reach the

*Downtown was always beautifully decked out for Christmas.*

62

pull cord, so I had to ask my customer to yank on the cord so the sales slip and cash would soar upwards. Most of my customers seemed quite willing. Then we both had to wait until the cup came back down, with the sales slip copy marked "sold" and any change inside. I quickly learned the art of chit chat.

Unlike my older sister, Kay, I actually enjoyed working in the store, watching how merchandise was unpacked and steam pressed before it was put on hangers and sent to its specific department, windows were "dressed," and merchandise in the counters arranged and rearranged to look more enticing. (One of our window dressers was a man named Syd Solomon, who later made a quite name for himself as a well-known and successful oil painting artist.)

Kay ignored our father's merchandise (that could have been bought at wholesale prices or even at cost) and preferred buying her clothes at retail at Younkers, the competing department store. It drove my father crazy by her saying so. I didn't care that much about fashion or what I wore and let my mother select my clothes (at cost or wholesale) throughout my college days.

I loved the Christmas spirit surrounding the shoppers, the Santa Clauses who came into the store to get warm when it was snowing, the music (many songs, including "White Christmas," written by Irving Berlin, a fellow Jew), and the feeling that I was "grown up" as I earned a little cash from my father for my efforts.

Occasionally, a man would wander into the store, often unshaven, wearing snow stained shoes, dressed in a worn and slightly torn overcoat, and a soiled felt fedora. He, like the others he resembled who had preceded him, would remove his hat and ask for my father. I'd locate Daddy on the floor or if he was in his office and escort the man to him. It happened often during the holiday season with a variety of men, some old and some young. Although each was different in his own way, each wore clothes that had seen better days and looked tired.

One evening, on the way home from work, I asked Daddy who these various men were. He told me they were fellow Jews who had fallen on hard times. "They're *shnorers'*," he said, using a Yiddish expression to mean beggars. "They can't find jobs right now."

63

"What do they want with you?"

"They need a helping hand," he told me softly. "I give them some money to help them pull themselves up."

"You give them money?" I asked in surprise.

He nodded. "They'd do the same for me if our situations were reversed. Jews need to be able to count on fellow Jews."

# CHAPTER 14: STAGE STRUCK

*"Every now and then, when you're on stage,*
*you hear the best sound a player can hear…*
*It is the sound of a wonderful, deep silence*
*that means you've hit them where they live."*
Shelley Winters,
Theatre Arts, June 1956

I guess you never lose the scent of grease paint. I always loved acting and still do. My sophomore year of high school, I was cast in the senior class play called *Cash and Carrie*. I played the eleven-year-old daughter and probably had been cast only because I was small and fit into the Girl Scout uniform that was important to the plot.

Later that year, I gave a monologue for drama class and the teacher, Mr. Waterman, asked if I had any other "pieces" I could perform. He had a request from the Gold Star Mothers for someone to entertain at a luncheon at the end of the week. The Gold Star Mothers were women who had lost a son in World War II. They had flags with a gold star that they placed in the window of their home. Naturally, I assured my instructor that I had many such pieces and agreed to appear at the luncheon.

Then I ran home and asked my mother to write something for me. She had been a newspaper reporter after graduating from The Ohio State University and was a good writer. She quickly wrote a number of pieces and we selected two of them. We rehearsed them over and over until I had memorized them and we both felt comfortable that they were performance ready.

The day of the luncheon, I was excused from school to do my good deed. Mother dropped me off, said she'd come back in an hour, and wished me luck. With butterflies in my stomach, I walked into the luncheon. The women were just finishing up and were drinking coffee, and eating cake. The president of the organization introduced me, the clanking of cups and silverware quieted, and I stood up, took a big breath, and began, remembering my father's direction to find three people in the audience—one on the left, one in the back middle, and one on the right and speak to them. Both of the recital pieces that mother had written were humorous and fortunately, they were received that way.

After the applause, I surprised myself by saying, "For my final piece, I'd like to include one that may be familiar to you." With that, I began to recite from memory one of A.A. Milne's poems I've always loved, called "Vespers." It begins with, "Little boy kneels at the foot of his bed…" When I finished, there was silence. I panicked. Had I messed up? Then I heard sniffs and a few sobs, and noticed that the women were digging into their purses for their handkerchiefs and wiping their eyes. They all stood up and applauded, then came up to the platform and hugged me. I was hooked!

That poem became my signature final piece with all the women's groups for which I performed. Sometimes it was for the Gold Star Mothers, but often for various Christian women's groups who had heard of the "little Jewish girl" who recited.

# CHAPTER 15:
# JEWISH ATHLETE PERSONIFIED
# AND OTHER JUNIOR HIGH MEMORIES

*"I failed to make the chess team because of my height."*
Woody Allen

In my mind, I'm an athlete. This fantasy is somewhat akin to singing in the shower with the bold assurance that you can really carry a tune. I've always loved the idea of playing sports. But I'm what is known as a klutz. I was hit in the eye playing softball (and first discovered that I was very nearsighted in the other eye and needed glasses) and kicked in the knee playing kickball, thus causing a locked or "trick knee," that does no tricks other than occasionally locking on me.

When I got to junior high, however, the idea of gym classes did not sound very inviting. The girls' required gym outfits were ugly and baggy and we had to take showers after the class. We were given only one skimpy towel that was effective in only covering just one area at a time. Unfortunately, there were only so many times a month a girl could confide to the coach that she had her period and could she please be excused.

*It was only for a skit I had written, but it was fun being a football player even briefly.*

So, I took the only other way out. I fell back on the "I had rheumatic fever" plea and finally was permanently excused from the physical education requirement. From then on, my "sports" included competitive ping pong (I was junior high school champion one year) and checkers (ditto).

*Fort Dodge Junior High School, now Fair Oaks Middle School.*

But in ninth grade, I finally I had the urge to use my gym shoes. I entered a basketball free throw contest. Over a set period of weeks, the contestants had to throw a total of 100 free throws under the watchful eye of the gym teacher. I'm sure that my record still stands. Out of 100 free throws, I managed to not make one single basket. The ball usually fell sadly short.

I was in seventh grade when my only foray into politics occurred. We had just "moved up" from grade school and were told it was time to hold elections for seventh grade officers. A couple of the more popular kids said they would run for president and vice-president, so I decided to run for treasurer. My opponent was Charles LaFrance, an African-American young man from one of the other elementary schools so I didn't know him. But, as he seemed friendly, I voted for him, thinking it would have been immodest to vote for myself! He won the election, which was probably just as well as I'm dyslexic with numbers. Charles and I remained friends throughout our junior high years.

I did, however, become the unofficial president of the Quad C Club in Junior High. That stood for "Crazy Color Combination of Clothes Club." The members were challenged to come up with the nuttiest outfits, mixing plaids with stripes and orange with reds and pinks. It was fun for a while, but somehow the club disbanded when we all were promoted into eighth grade and boys started to look more interesting.

# CHAPTER 16: WRITING'S RIGHT

*"When it is obvious that the goals cannot be reached,*
*do not adjust the goals, adjust the action steps."*
Confucius

Once I learned how to write, it was always my strong suit. At eight, I had no present for my mother for her birthday, January 1st and was already in debt having to borrow two weeks allowance to buy Christmas presents. Undaunted, I presented her with the only original copy of *Good Short Stories* by Elaine Carol Fantle. (Yes, I still have it!)

My sister sneered, "How do you know they're any good?"

"Well," I answered. "At least they're short." They were about "Bobby and Betty," who went sledding and Betty broke her arm and then they formed a club; "Tom," who had ten brothers and ten sisters and got a doctor kit for his birthday; "Carol" who had hurt her leg and could not walk; and "Tom, The Teacher's Pet" who 'caught a cold and it was mumps.' You may notice a common theme here. This might have been the beginning of why I became a medical writer.

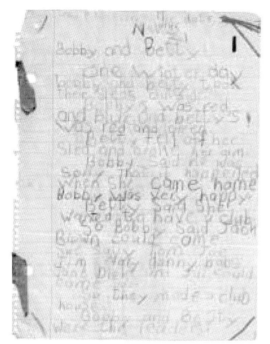

*My first "published" book for my mother's birthday was* **Good Short Stories** *by Elaine Carol Fantle.*

In third grade, during World War II, we all sent letters to anonymous "G.I. Joes." One day, to my surprise, I was called up to the teacher's desk and handed a "V-mail" (short for "Victory Mail"). It was a copy of a letter, microfilmed to save cargo space and reduced in size to 4 1/4x5 inches. It was from a Sergeant Arch Thorson, who thanked me for writing to him. Although I don't know what happened to that precious piece of history, I've never forgotten his name and have thought about him often over these many years.

To my surprise, while writing this, I learned that Archie Thorson actually was from Fort Dodge. I called information and got the name of a good friend of his, Sherwin Thorson (no relation). He told me that although Archie had passed away, his daughter still lived in Fort Dodge. I was saddened to know that until 1982 when he died, I could have spoken with my "G.I. Joe" and let him know what he had meant to me by simply writing a letter to an eight year old.

*I finally "found" the GI Joe who had written to me in the third grade. Alas, it wasn't until he was deceased. Archie Thorson played banjo in his band.*

Archie's daughter, Sherri Josephson, told me that Archie had played the banjo in his Dixie Land Kings band. They once had performed for then President Ronald Reagan. "My father was gentle, easygoing, and fun-loving," she said. "He loved music and like his father, he played the banjo by ear." Archie sounded just like the person who had written to me so long ago and I was sorry I had never located him before he died at age sixty-four.

In sixth grade, we studied about China. Rather than doing a term paper, I decided to write a play. It was called *Death in the Rice Fields* and consisted of my reluctant cast running into the adjacent cloak room one by one and screaming as they died. It was a major success in that I got an "A" on it.

In junior high, we had to write a paper on "How a Bill Becomes a Law." For some unknown reason, I decided to write it as a poem. When the teacher handed the papers back, mine had no grade, just the note, "See me after class."

I thought that perhaps she wasn't happy about my writing it in poetry. Instead, she picked up the paper and said, "Where did you get this?"

"Get what?" I asked.

"This poem," she answered, waving it in my face.

"I wrote it," I said. "You didn't say I couldn't write it in poetry."

"YOU wrote it?" she asked again, and to my great embarrassment, my eyes started to fill. I always was a crier. She continued to question me until finally, it must have sunk in that I actually had written it. "Well, good," she said. "I just had to be sure you hadn't copied it from some book."

She gave me an "A" but I took no pleasure in the grade. It was the first and only time I have ever been accused of plagiarism. It hurt and the fact that I still recall the incident, shows that it still smarts.

In ninth grade, my report card showed an "A" in English. The teacher had written, "Elaine shows talent in writing." She told me that she thought I could become a professional writer if I wanted to. It just demonstrates the power of a teacher's encouragement. Her name was Caroline Longfellow and we corresponded for many years afterwards. I still have one of her last letters. It began, as did the others, with "Ma chere."

*High School. I loved that coat!*

73

My sophomore year of high school, the Chamber of Commerce ran an essay contest for students to answer the question, "What the Bill of Rights Means to Me?" I won that contest by comparing it to what the Ten Commandments meant to me as a Jewish person. Up until then, I had never thought of myself as being particularly religious, but the essay almost wrote itself. Obviously, some of what those dedicated mothers had tried to teach me in the shabby two-room religious school over Constantine's Restaurant on Sunday mornings had sunk in. I never knew if the "brilliance" of my essay had swayed the judges or if it had been the only essay they received from a Jew and that fact alone had been the deciding factor. I prefer to think it was the former.

I first became a "professional writer," in that I was paid, by winning an essay contest sponsored by the Real Estate Board. The first prize was $25 dollars. I thought then and still think that it's great to be paid for doing what you really love.

# CHAPTER 17: MATZO BALL MEMORIES

*"As a child, my family's menu consisted of two choices:*
*Take it or leave it."*
Buddy Hackett

Jewish cuisine is supposed to be memorable. At least most of my Jewish friends wax eloquently about their grandmother's and mother's cooking. But I think a woman has to enjoy cooking to earn those kudos. Mother really didn't like to cook which was fine with Daddy because by his own admission, he only "ate to live." He was just as happy with scrambled eggs for dinner as steak. I wasn't. I loved to cook and loved to eat. Still do. In fact, he often declared that I could eat more than he. I thought that was a positive as a kid; as an adult, it is the reason for my constant diets.

To be fair, my mother did cook two things well. She made a great pumpkin pie for Thanksgiving and since her death, I have never found anyone who could make it as tasty and she made an excellent stew. As you quickly discern, she did not "cook Jewish."

As we were Reform (as were our grandparents on both sides), we didn't keep kosher (the dietary laws or *kashrut*) at our house. I don't know how anyone in Fort Dodge could have as we didn't even have a deli, but as some did, they must have "ordered in" from Des Moines. Until I was eighteen, I had never tasted, let alone heard of blintzes, kugel, knishes, kreplach, gefilte fish, potato latkes, borscht, schnecken (yeast raised sweet rolls), tsimmes, or pastrami. I had sampled hamantaschen (pastry stuffed with a prune or apricot mixture) because one of the other women made it for the religious school at Purim. It was shaped in a triangle, like Haman's hat and, of course, I had enjoyed the matzo ball soup that my mother made from a mix.

When I got to Northwestern, my classmates were appalled to hear of my deprived childhood. They dragged me to the "El" and we rode from Evanston to Morse Avenue in Chicago.

"This," said my mentor proudly, "is Ashkenaz, a delicatessen magnifique."

"It's home," mumbled someone from Shaker Heights.

The aroma of dill hit me first and I almost tripped over a giant vat filled with small cucumbers.

"These are Kosher Dills," said my mentor. "Repeat after me. 'Kosher Dills.'"

I intoned the liturgy. This was one language course I was going to enjoy.

They obviously had committed the giant menu to heart, ordering bagels, cream cheese, and lox, latkes, gefilte fish, kugel, knishes, kreplach, and knaidlach. The latter sounded like a new singing group to me. Someone handed me a Kosher Dill. I took a bite. My mouth watered. It crunched. What an assortment of textures there were. The crisp firm, yet somewhat bumpy outside hid the surprise of chewy seeds inside and the lingering flavor of dill and vinegar... always that marvelous smell and of dill. We washed everything down with Dr. Brown's Cream Soda.

Although I've been back to Chicago, I never returned to Ashkenaz. I believe it moved to Ceder Street. Yet the pungent smell of dill is still sweeter to me than any perfume. I'm thinking of bottling a Jewish furniture polish and calling it "Kosher Dill Wax." Like Proust and his "madeleine" dipped in tea in *Swann's Way*, aromas do bring back remembrances of things past. I'll always remember how I came of age at "Ashkies."

# CHAPTER 18: MOVING TO THE "BIG CITY"

*"I have been a stranger in a strange land."*
Exodus 2:22

Okay, so Sioux City, Iowa really was not a strange land, but when you're sixteen and in the last half of your junior year of high school, and your parents tell you that you're moving to a new town over the summer, that place seems very strange and scary. Apparently, my father was taking over the management of the Fantle Brothers store in Sioux City although I had heard no discussion of it at the dinner table and no one had asked or cared about my opinion on the subject.

I was not happy and that fact was probably why my parents had never asked me how I felt about it. Parents then were not so concerned about their children's psyche. I was leaving behind friends I had known since kindergarten—Carolyn McCoy, Georgeann Whittemore, and Frank "Butch" Waldburger, not to mention my boyfriend, Bruce, (who immediately got swooped up by my competitor). In addition, I was losing the opportunity to be editor of the high school paper my senior year. (As it turned out, I actually did become editor of the Sioux City Central High School paper my senior year.)

Sioux City had three times the population of Fort Dodge and had enough Jews to support a Reform temple, a Conservative synagogue, and a deli as well. It also had a large enough Jewish population that there were a number of interesting Jewish boys to date. But when school started in the fall, the first few weeks felt awkward without seeing any familiar faces.

Daddy had bought a home in the Country Club section of Sioux City, not realizing that no other Jewish families lived there. In the beginning, I rode the school bus and developed a nodding acquaintance with the other riders. Soon, my father bought a new car for himself and gave me his old car. It was a 1949 two-door yellow and black Cadillac. I named it "Tiger Lil" and although I was delighted to have "wheels" and not have to ride the bus anymore, I was embarrassed to be driving a "Caddie." I tried, unsuccessfully, to convince my schoolmates that Tiger Lil was a Buick that had been mismarked.

I was the "new girl in town." The boys liked that; the girls did not. They had already formed their cliques. Eventually, I began dating (only Jewish boys as the Gentile ones didn't ask me). Slowly, I began to get involved in activities at school, being careful not to talk about how things were done in Fort Dodge. I signed up for *The Record*, the high school newspaper and began writing features, becoming its editor my senior year. I joined various clubs including the Dramatics Club, Pep Club, the Friendship Club, and the Red Cross. I served as president of the Spanish Club.

Yet my major involvement was with the Sioux City Community Little Theater. I was their primary ingénue for the year and a half I was still in high school.

It was there in Sioux City that I first realized how assimilated I had been in Fort Dodge. It happened during my first Passover there when I noticed a number of my Jewish classmates eating sandwiches at lunch made with matzo, rather than bread.

"Why are you doing that?" I asked one of the more friendly girls. "The Seder was three days ago."

She looked at me curiously. "What kind of a Jew are you?" she asked. "You're supposed to eat matzo instead of bread all during Passover, not just for the Seder."

Oops. I tried, unsuccessfully, to hide my bologna sandwich nestled in Wonder Bread slathered in Miracle Whip.

A 1st century B.C. Roman poet and actor, Publilius Syrus, was the first to say, "Familiarity breeds contempt." He was right. In Sioux City, the Reform Jews socialized primarily with their own as did the Conservatives. Each synagogue had their own youth group and there wasn't a great deal of fraternization. I joined the Mount Sinai Temple Youth Group and MOFTY (The Missouri Federation of Temple Youth) which included Reform Jewish young people from Iowa, Missouri, Kansas, Illinois (other than Chicago), and Nebraska. Later, Colorado and Wyoming were included. I was delighted to learn that we had meetings in Des Moines, Omaha, and Lincoln where we met more Jewish (Reform, only) young people (i.e. boys). There also were local groups where both Reform and Conservative youths could meet, called Aleph Zadik Aleph (AZA) and B'nai B'rith Girls (BBG). There even was a Jewish Community Center where Eddie, a boy I was dating, played basketball.

*The "Castle" high on the hill was overwhelming at first, but I quickly learned to love it.*

After completing the remainder of my junior and senior year in Sioux City, I graduated from Sioux City Central High, known as "The Castle," because it resembled a Norman castle. Graduation was a somewhat anticlimactic event. I had been a mid-year student which meant we graduated in January, not June. We had no festive prom and if there were other private parties, I was not invited. That evening I went out with Syd, a young (Jewish) baker I was seeing.

Although I had worked my way up to being the editor of the high school paper (as I was to have been in Fort Dodge), I really had made only a few close girlfriends in school, mostly just friends. Surprisingly, however, I was selected as one of the dozen "All For Central" students for the Maroon and White yearbook. I never knew if it was the faculty or students who selected those candidates.

Then, and even now, my heart and fondest girlhood memories were still in Fort Dodge.

*My high school graduation picture. Note the pearls. Every girl wore pearls!*

# EPILOGUE

Did "living in a small town without many Jewish families" have an effect on me? I'm sure it did. It made me realize that everyone's different in some way and that's okay. (In fact, I recently wrote a children's book called Helga, The Hippopotamouse. She was part hippo and part mouse and, of course, that made her different. In the end, Helga realizes that all the other animals are different too.)

As my "watchword" taught, I learned to be content with whatever gifts God had given to me and to share these gifts—by my writing, caring for others, listening ability, sense of humor, and philanthropic opportunities. Certainly, my growing up years in Fort Dodge helped to make me the woman I am today.

Sadly, our synagogue in Fort Dodge, like so many others in small communities is no more. It closed in 1998. The building still stands on 501 North 12th Street, but it now is the youth center for the Presbyterian Church across the street. It was renamed "The Shalom Center."

I haven't been back to Fort Dodge since I left it as a sixteen year old. I hope to return when this book is published to see "old" friends. But I know the scenery will be far different than I remember. Lincoln School, my former elementary school, was torn down in 1956 and is now an athletic field. The building that once housed my father's former store burned down in 1972 and has been replaced by the First Federal Savings and Loan. And sadly, our magnificent home that held so many memories for me sustained major fire damage on February 20, 1977 and had to be torn down.

I know Thomas Wolfe said, "You can't go home again," but you can, you know, if only in your mind.

*"Teach me, O Lord,*
*to obey Thy will,*
*to be content with what,*
*in Thy wisdom,*
*Thou hast allotted to me, and to share Thy gifts*
*with those who need my help."*

# ABOUT THE AUTHOR

Elaine Fantle Shimberg is the author of 22 books and five children's books. She authored a column for *THE JEWISH FLORIDIAN OF TAMPA* for two years and has written the history for the 75th anniversary book for Shriners' Children's Hospitals and the 100th anniversary history of her temple, Congregation Schaarai Zedek in Tampa. She is the unofficial historian of the Straz Center for the Performing Arts (formerly the Tampa Bay Performing Arts).

Her books include subjects on blending families and other family issues, writing, and health care subjects ranging from strokes, depression, and irritable bowel syndrome to Tourette Syndrome, heartburn, and gastric reflux disease. She has appeared on the "TODAY" show and "AM CHICAGO" as well as many radio shows and is the author of numerous magazine articles in *Reader's Digest*, *Glamour*, *Seventeen*, *Woman's Day*, and others.

For five years she co-hosted a women's talk show on WFLA-TV in Tampa. In 2002, she received an honorary Doctor of Humane Letters degree from the University of South Florida. She is a member of the American Society of Journalists and Authors (ASJA) and is the past president of the Florida Chapter of the American Medical Writers Association (AMWA).

Shimberg, a Northwestern graduate, is married, lives in Tampa, Florida, and spends her summers in Maine. She has five adult children and ten grandchildren. Her website is www.ElainesBooks.com.

Special thanks to:

**Roger B. Natte**, Fort Dodge Historian, who helped me tremendously by finding photos to help illustrate sections of my book; Fort Dodge **Dave Marrs,** for still considering me part of the Fort Dodge High School Class of 1955 and keeping me aware of class news; **Alan A. Arkin,** my brother-in-law, for his insights; **Marvin Barkin** for sharing some of what his life in a small town was like; **Mimi Swartz Keller**, one of my confirmation classmates, for her remembrances; **Fr. Richard Graves**, for suggesting I contact Roger Natte; **Bud Levinger**, my cousin, for helping me with family history; **Jerry Higgins, Marie Killinger, Sandy Rogers May, Harlene Glazer Lewin, and Frank "Butch" Waldburger** for remembrances of Fort Dodge and taking time to answer my questions; **Georgeann Whittemore Kuhl**, for remembrances of Fort Dodge and forgiving me for scaring her with a worm; **Webster Country Historical Society** archives for allowing me to use their wonderful photos; **Harold Bergeman**, photographer; **Sherry Thorson** for sharing photos of her dad, Archie Thorson, and telling me about him; **Isaac Mallah**, my friend of almost thirty years, for his photo shop expertise and touching up old photos; **Veronica Tillis**, for proofreading (any typos were added after she did her work!); **Sandy Walling**, my editor and friend; **Rabbi Richard Birnholz**, for always being there; **Ginny Saunders** of Abernathy House Publishing for all her help and patience; and **Gallery Studio of Tampa** for the author's photo.

# Suggested Reading

Edward Cohen, *The Peddler's Son: Growing Up Jewish in Mississippi* (University Press of Mississippi) 1999

Howard V. Epstein, *Jews in Small Towns: Legends and Legacies* (Vision Books International) 1997

Eli N. Evans, *The Loneliest Days Were Sundays: Reflections of a Jewish Southerner* (Free Press Paperbacks, Simon & Schuster) 1973, 1977

Eli N. Evans, *The Provincials: A Personal History of Jews in the South* (Free Press Paperbacks, Simon & Schuster) 1973, 1977

Abram Leon Sacher, Ph.D., *A History of the Jews* (New York: Alfred Knopf) 1967

Charles Silberman, *A Certain People* (New York: Summit Books) 1985

Lee Shai Weissbach, *Jewish Life in Small-Town America* (Yale University Press) 2005

# INDEX

# ALSO BY ELAINE FANTLE SHIMBERG

*The Complete Single Father: Reassuring Answers to Your Most Challenging Situations*

*Another Chance for Love: Finding a Partner Later in Life*

Coping with COPD: Understanding, Treating, and Living with Chronic Obstructive Pulmonary Disease

Coping with Chronic Heartburn: What You Need to Know About Acid Reflux and GERD

Write Where You Live: Successful Freelancing at Home

Blending Families: A Guide for Parents, Stepparents, and Everyone Building a Successful New Family

*How to Get Out of the Hospital Alive*

Living with Tourette Syndrome

*Gifts of Time*

Depression: What Families Should Know

Strokes: What Families Should Know

Relief from IBS: Irritable Bowel Syndrome

*Coping with Kids and Vacation*

*Two for the Money: A Woman's Guide to a Double Career Marriage*

How to Be a Successful Housewife/Writer

**Children's Books**

The Boys' Adventure Club of Maine

Emily Goes to Camp Lobster Claw

Max, The Magical Moose

Herman, The Hermit Crab

Helga, The Hippopotamouse

**\*co-authored**

Municipal Band Shell, Oleson Park, Fort Dodge, Iowa

*Waiting for the movie at the Rialto.*

*The High School in Fort Dodge.*

*Kay and I out for a ride around the "Big House" yard.*

*Constructed in 1902, the style of the courthouse set the tone for Fort Dodge building for the next 15 years.*

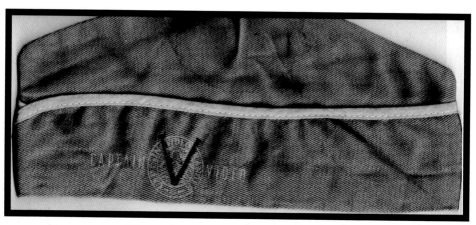

*The much coveted "Captain Video" hat.*

*Giant Malts for 25¢, Fort Dodge, Iowa.*

*The Exposition Pool built in 1925. An excellent place to be on a hot summer day.*

# Questions for Discussion

1. Author Elaine Fantle Shimberg is best known for writing books on health subjects and family issues. Why do you think she decided to write her memoir?

2. Elaine goes into great detail describing the house in which she grew up. Why was that so important to her? Do you have a home in your past that was meaningful?

3. Although Elaine's religious education was a mixture of Bible stories, holiday pageants, and a few specific prayers told by teachers who were mothers, she describes a particular prayer as the "watchword" for her. Why was it so meaningful for her? Do you have a special prayer that guides your daily life?

4. Why was Elaine's mother so upset by the fourth grade teacher reading from the New Testament? Could her mother have handled the situation more satisfactorily?

5. Elaine describes her childhood experience with stealing. Do you think it was handled properly?

6. Elaine mentions a teacher who had a great effect on her choice of career. Describe a teacher who effected your life—either positively or negatively.

7. Does Elaine present information in a way that is interesting and insightful, and if so, how does she achieve this?

8. What one new fact did you learn from reading this book?